Book2Web™

Making Sense of Sound and Music

By Eileen Giuffré Cotton and Carole F. Stice

Making Sense of Sound and Music

Vibrations
Rapid movement makes sound.
Page 4

When Noise Becomes Music
What makes the difference?
Page 10

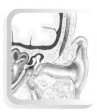

Sneezes, Thunder, Sirens
Each sound has its own characteristics.
Page 6

Do, Re, Mi
What is the basis for Western music?
Page 12

Real-Life Sound Effects
Sound is always making waves.
Page 8

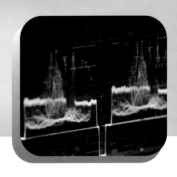

www.book2web.com

Vibrations

Something has to vibrate to make a sound. It is that simple. Stretch a rubber band really tight and then pluck it. You can see the rubber band vibrating. Once a vibration starts, air (a medium) carries the vibrations away from the rubber band (a source). The vibrating rubber band pushes against the air molecules next to it. The molecules closest to the rubber band are knocked into the next set of air molecules. Those molecules bump the ones next to them and so on. All this vibration reaches your ears very quickly. Your eardrums start to vibrate, too. And your brain says, "Aha, a sound! It's a hum." You see the vibrating rubber band, and you know where the humming sound came from.

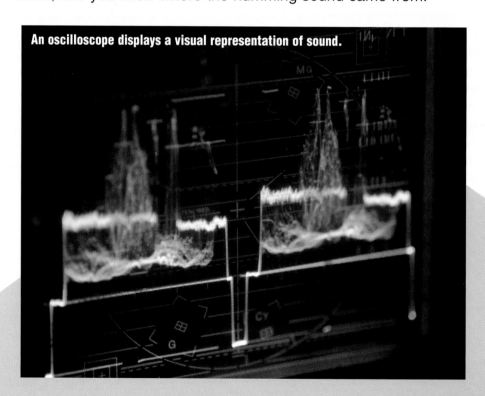

An oscilloscope displays a visual representation of sound.

There is no sound in space.

Hot Sounds
Sound travels faster in warm air than in cold air. Molecules collide with one another more often in warm air than in cold air, so they transmit sound faster.

▲ Vacuums Suck Up Sound
Sound cannot travel in a vacuum. It needs something elastic, such as air or water, to carry it along. You couldn't really hear a spaceship or a comet pass by in space. That only happens in the movies. Space is a vacuum and very quiet indeed.

Dense Air
Dense air carries vibrations more easily than thin air. Air in valleys is denser—the molecules are closer together—than air on mountaintops. So you can hear better in a valley than on a mountain.

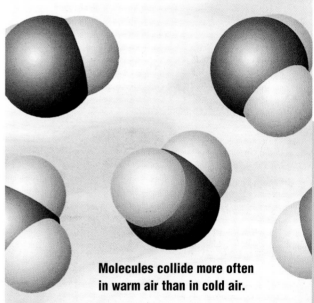

Molecules collide more often in warm air than in cold air.

Find Out More

Sound does not travel at the same speed in gases (like air), liquids, and solids. In which of these media do you think sound travels the fastest? Why? To find out more, go to

book2web.com

5

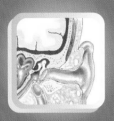

Sneezes, Thunder, Sirens

When we hear a dog barking, we know without looking what is making the noise. We distinguish a sound by its loudness, pitch, or quality. Loudness is a measure of the size of a sound's vibrations in the air. The farther you pull a rubber band back before you let it go, the greater the distance of its back-and-forth motion will be and the louder the sound will be.

If you stretch the rubber band tighter, the sound it makes will be higher. Pitch describes how high or how low a sound is. The faster something vibrates, the higher its pitch will be.

We also distinguish sounds by their quality. No sounds, except some electronic ones, are absolutely pure. The sound of a clarinet and a trombone playing the same note equally loud is not the same. The brass of a trombone and the wood in a clarinet's reed produce different mixtures of vibrations. These mixtures of vibrations make a sound unique.

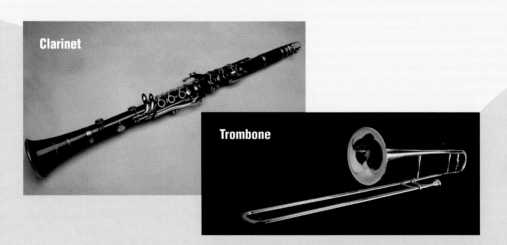

Clarinet

Trombone

Dolphins have keen ultrasound hearing.

Ultrasound A sound's frequency—the number of vibrations of the sound wave per second—is measured in hertz. We hear frequencies as low as twenty hertz, which is a lower frequency than our voices can make, and as high as twenty thousand hertz. Ultrasound is frequencies higher than twenty thousand hertz. Although dogs and other animals can hear ultrasound, dolphins and bats have the keenest ultrasound hearing.

Bels Loudness—or sound intensity—is usually measured in decibels. The bel is the basic unit of measurement for intensity. The word *bel* honors Alexander Graham Bell, who invented the telephone. *Deci* means ten.

Flexible Ears Our ears are remarkable. We can hear sounds a million times softer than the level of normal talking. But loud noises can harm our ears. Sound that is too loud, such as a jet engine or even loud music, can damage a person's hearing.

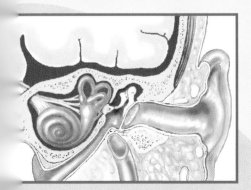

Find Out More

Every object has its own natural frequency. If you drop a coin on the floor, the sound is different from a pen falling on the floor or a hat falling on the floor. Why do different objects make different sounds? To find out more, go to

book2web.com

Real-Life Sound Effects

I f you touch your finger to water in a cup, little waves travel to the cup's wall and then bounce back. Sound, like water, also moves as a wave and bounces back from a wall. This is an echo. If you made a noise in an empty hallway, you might hear an echo.

Sound can also cause objects to vibrate or resonate. Each object has a natural frequency of vibration. When you make a sound near an object at that object's natural frequency, the object might rattle or move a little. That is, it vibrates. This kind of vibration caused by a sound is called resonance.

Sound also changes as its source moves. As a police car speeds by, the pitch of its siren seems to drop. This is called the Doppler effect. The pitch seems to change because the sound's source is moving, not because the frequency has changed.

▲ **Echo** Echo Echo Sound in well-designed rooms is rich and lively but still easy to hear. If a large room reflects sound too well, music or voices bounce back and forth. Everything sounds jumbled.

Find Out More

Dolphins use ultrasound. They rely on echoes to locate and identify objects in the sea, including their next meal. They might even see the outlines and bones of other animals. How do dolphins do this? To find out more, go to

book2web.com

Echo Sounding Surveyors and scientists use sound to map the ocean floor. A ship sends out a sound and then records the time it takes for the reflected wave (echo) to get back. Scientists know the speed sound travels in water, so they can calculate the ocean's depth or the distance to an underwater object.

Bending Sound Although we cannot see around corners, we can hear around corners. Sound travels in all directions from its source. Sound also travels at different speeds—faster in warm air and slower in cold air.

When Noise Becomes Music

Music to one person might be noise to someone else; noise to one culture might be music to another. What sounds please you? In the United States, most people agree that music is sound made with regular vibrations. Such a sound is a tone, which is a part of music. Vibrations are easy to measure. An oscilloscope is an electronic instrument that displays pictures of sound wave forms on a screen. This shows whether the vibrations are regular.

Tones are an important part of music and may help separate music from noise. But that does not tell us what music is. The way tones are put together and the way music makes people feel separate it from noise. These characteristics cannot be measured and are hard to explain. Music causes and communicates emotions. Music can give us goose bumps, make us sad, make us happy, fill us full of energy, and much more. It is the love of this side of music that all people, everywhere, share.

▼ Noise to Music Many sounds are pleasing even if they are not made with regular vibrations. Sounds people associate with an enjoyable experience, such as the sound of waves washing up on a beach, make those sounds seem pleasant.

Pitch and Partials Sounds made by musical instruments contain more than one tone. Each tone has a definite vibration and pitch (how high or low a note is). The lowest and most dominant tone is called the fundamental tone. The other tones that make up an instrument's characteristic sound are called partials.

▲ Music to Noise Many sounds are disturbing to us even if they have regular vibrations. Any sound can be an unpleasant noise if it is too loud. Even music, if it reminds us of something we do not like, can be unpleasant.

Find Out More

Suppose you were friends with someone in a civilization just like ours on another planet. Your communications were only with pictures. How would you explain the difference between music and noise to your friend? To find out more, go to

book2web.com

Do, Re, Mi

A composer organizes tones to create music. The first step is to name a pitch as the keynote; that is, a home base. This is the "do" in "do, re, mi, fa, sol, la, ti, do." The rest of the tones in the sequence are the family of the keynote. Together these notes make a musical scale. Each note in the scale has a letter, and sometimes another symbol, to identify it. The range in pitches of these notes make up an octave. If an octave is rising, it ends with a pitch twice as high as the keynote. In the system used in the United States and other Western countries, the octave is traditionally divided into twelve equal steps.

do, re, mi, fa, sol, la, ti, do

It's the Key Each of the twelve notes of an octave on a piano (seven white keys and five black keys) is a half tone apart. Are there black keys missing? No. There is only a half tone between each of the two pairs of white keys that do not have a black key between them.

Seven Notes Although we see eight notes on a musical staff, only seven are used at one time in a scale. It doesn't matter what note we start on. It is still "do, re, mi, fa, sol, la, ti, do." The last "do" is the repeat of the keynote at the start of the next higher octave. That leaves seven.

Scales Musical scales developed in different ways around the world. Western culture uses a half-tone scale with twelve tones. Asian music uses a scale with five tones. Arabic music uses seventeen tones. Traditional music in India is based on quarter-tones. Each culture developed musical instruments on which to play its traditional music.

Find Out More

Two notes that are one octave apart on a piano make a pleasant sound when played at the same time. Why do you think this is? To find out more, go to

book2web.com

From Tones to Tunes

Tones organized into keynotes and scales are the basic building blocks of music. A composer uses these to write a melody, which is the heart of a piece of music. The melody is what we remember about a song; it is what we hum. A melody has a wonderful quality. It is just a series of tones, but that series of tones seems to have a beginning, a middle, and an end. It also has a personality.

A melody needs more than tones. A composer must also decide how to control the flow of the tones—when to play each note and how long to keep playing it. This is the part of music we call rhythm. It makes us want to move around. The notes and rhythm create a melody.

Finally, the composer might add harmony. Harmony is the chords (notes played together) that support the melody. Harmony gives music depth and richness.

◄ Want to Learn Languages? Music is written in a very foreign language. Sheet music looks like horizontal lines, vertical lines with balls on the end, dots, and squiggles. Italian, German, and French words written all over the page give directions. The amazing thing is that people all over the world can read music. It's not hard to learn!

► A Basic Chord A basic type of chord is the triad. This is a special group of three notes played together. Starting with "do," a triad could be the "do, mi, sol" notes. On a piano this chord can be made with the three white keys C, E, and G.

Name That Tune Melodies are part of our global heritage. When one person starts humming or singing a melody, sometimes it seems that everyone knows it. Maybe they will join in. Many melodies are popular and known around the world. Melodies help bind us together.

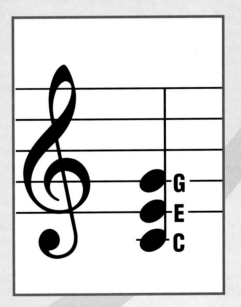

Find Out More

The conductor could talk to the orchestra instead of waving a baton. Which method do you think would work better? Why? To find out more, go to

book2web.com

The Music Makers

What turns a melody written on paper into something we can hear? How do we make music? We use stringed instruments, wind instruments, percussion, and singing.

Stringed instruments make music when their strings vibrate from bowing, strumming, or plucking. The length of a vibrating string controls the pitch, or note. A musician changes the length of the string by pressing the string against the fingerboard at the correct spot.

To play a wind instrument (woodwind or brass), a musician makes a column of air vibrate. The musician shortens or lengthens this column to play a specific note by blowing and covering holes in the column (clarinets and flutes), or pressing valves (trumpets).

Percussion instruments make sounds when struck. The world's many percussion instruments include drums, cymbals, xylophones, and gongs.

The world's favorite way to make music is by singing. We control the vibration of our vocal chords to sing different notes. Usually we don't even think about our vocal chords; we just sing.

◀ **Blow!** To play most wind instruments, the musician needs to blow continuously to keep making music. But bagpipes store air that the piper squeezes out of the bag as it is needed. Native Australians play an instrument called the bullroarer. They whirl it around their heads to make sounds like wind and storms.

Piano The piano and its cousins the harpsichord and clavichord are special percussion instruments that can play both melody and harmony. This makes them good instruments for soloists and ideal instruments for composing music.

▼ **String Section** Violins and other stringed instruments use a sounding board that amplifies vibrations. Normally, the sound of a string vibrating is not loud. When the thin sounding board of the instrument vibrates the same way the string vibrates, the sound is louder.

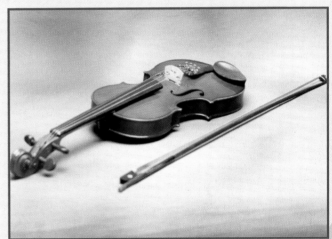

Find Out More

Every culture developed the same three basic types of instruments—string, wind, and percussion. Were they all created just to make music? What could an instrument be used for if not to make music? To find out more, go to

book2web.com

Electronic Music

Electronic music is more than sound coming out of a guitar attached to an electronic amplifier. Electronic systems that create—synthesize—sounds appeared in the early 1960s. These first synthesizers used an oscillator that made sound waves to replace sounds made by actual musical instruments. In the 1980s, digital synthesizers—computers that use numbers to represent musical notes or other sounds—became popular. In these systems, programmers mix sounds, create voices, copy familiar sounds, and make up new ones. You can make up a sound no one has ever heard before!

Composers can sit at a computer and write music using digitized sounds of musical instruments. They can then listen to the music, change it right at the computer, and listen to it again. The synthesizer provides all of the orchestra sounds. This is a big advantage. Bach, Beethoven, and Mozart would be amazed!

Max Mathews, one of the creators of the first music synthesizer

Wailing Music The theremin was one of the first electronic instruments. It was patented in 1928. A theremin makes an eerie, wailing sound that was featured in science fiction movies in the 1950s. It is the only instrument you can play without actually touching it.

Movie Music Music directors create unique sounds for motion pictures. The commercial synthesizers that they use have changed modern music.

▲ Compact Discs Digital audio technology brought compact discs—CDs—into our homes. Digital audio uses computer code instead of a tape recording. A laser reads the compact disc and doesn't touch its surface. That's why CDs won't wear out.

Find Out More

Electronic music can reproduce an entire orchestra or make a symphony from the sounds of falling leaves. If computers can be clarinets or an instrument no one ever heard before, why do we still use traditional musical instruments? To find out more, go to

book2web.com

19

Activities

Do something creative and share what you have learned from Book2Web. Each of these activities is about one of the topics in this book. You can use information you found while researching the Find Out More questions on book2web.com to do these projects.

Vibrations

Create a poster that shows the different speeds that sound travels through air, water, and metal.

Sneezes, Thunder, Sirens

Drop five small objects that differ in shape, size, or material a few inches onto a hard surface such as a desktop. Notice how the sounds are different. Decide the most important feature of an object for establishing its natural sound.

Real-Life Sound Effects

Learn the ways dolphins use sound. Now, pretend you are a famous author and write an action story in which a dolphin uses sound in all these ways to triumph.

When Noise Becomes Music

Listen to music or other recordings with your classmates. Make up a questionnaire including, "Did you like the recording?" and "What feelings did it bring to you?" Think of some other questions about music and noise for your questionnaire. Remember, there are no right or wrong answers. No two people react the same way to music. Look at the results and discuss them.

Do, Re, Mi

Try this on a piano with a few classmates: find middle C and play a scale to the next C. Strike each note and pause before going on. You play only the white keys. Now start the scale one note higher (D). What notes do you need to hit to make the scale sound right? Can you all agree?

From Tones to Tunes

Tempo is an important part of music. Choose a short song that everyone knows. Hum or sing the song at the regular speed. Next sing it twice as fast, then half as fast. Then change speeds in the middle in different ways. Write a paragraph on the effects of tempo.

The Music Makers

Look at materials in your classroom—paper, pencils, boxes, string, and so on. Draw a plan to use those materials to make a musical instrument. Show your plan to your teacher and get permission to build your instrument. What kind of sound does your instrument make? Is it a string, wind, or percussion instrument? What other purpose could your instrument serve?

Electronic Music

Computers allow us a new freedom to express ourselves through sound and music. Imagine that you attended a concert by a synthesizer. You are the music critic for your newspaper. Write a review of the performance.

Search Tips

The Web is a great place to find lots of information about almost any topic. But a search can take a long time. Here are some tips to make your searches on the Web and book2web.com faster and easier.

Brainstorming Words That Mean the Same Thing As Your Topic

The best way to search for information on the Web is to know all the words and phrases related to your topic, or words that mean the same thing as your topic. Make a list, or a word map, of these words. For example, if the search topic is planets, then some related words could be *solar system, outer space, space, world, Venus, Mercury, Earth, Mars, Jupiter, Saturn, Uranus, Neptune, Pluto, sun, moon,* and *universe.*

Now you can use these words to search for information on planets when you go to the Web or book2web.com.

Searching for a Word or Topic

What if you want to find out how big the planet Venus is? Then you want to look for Web pages that have the word *Venus*. For this kind of search, type the word in the search box like this:

| Venus | Search |

This will tell the search engine to look for Web pages with the word *Venus*.

Combining Search Words—Using AND

What if you want to search for information to compare the two planets Venus and Mars? Then you want to search for Web pages that have both of these words. For this kind of search, type the two words in the search box like this:

| Venus AND Mars | Search |

This will tell the search engine to look for Web pages with the words *Venus* and *Mars*.

Are all your search words spelled correctly? Always remember to check your spelling so the search engine can search for the right word.

Searching for Either One Word or Another— Using OR

What if you want to learn about Earth, and either of the words *Earth* or *world* would help you find out more about the topic? Then you want to search for Web pages that have either one of these words, or both words. For this kind of search, type the two words in the search box like this:

| Earth OR world | Search |

This will tell the search engine to look for Web pages with either the word *Earth* or the word *world*, or both words.

Keeping Words Out of Your Search—Using NOT

Do you keep seeing a word on the Web pages in your search that doesn't match your topic? For example, maybe you're searching for information about the planet Mars and you keep finding Web pages about the spacecraft *Mars Pathfinder*. To keep the word *Pathfinder* out of your search for Mars, type the two words in the search box like this:

| Mars NOT Pathfinder | Search |

This will tell the search engine to look for Web pages with the word *Mars* and not *Pathfinder*.

Searching with Web Links

The book2web.com home page has Web links that will take you to different parts of the book2web.com Web site. To find information using links, start by clicking on the first link you want to follow to find out more about your topic. Then look at the new list of links that appears. Find one link about your topic and click on that. Keep following the links until they take you to Web sites about the exact topic you want to research.

Even when you use these search tips, the Web pages you find may not have the information you need. Skim, or quickly read, the first part of the Web page to look for your search word or topic. If you see your search word or topic, the Web page may have the information you're looking for.

Glossary

decibel: The unit for measuring loudness.

Doppler effect: The frequency changes in a sound as the sound's source moves.

echo sounding: A technique of bouncing sound waves off objects and calculating distance from the speed of the returning sound.

frequency: The number of sound waves that pass a certain point in one second.

fundamental tone: The principal musical sound produced by vibration (as of a string or column of air).

hertz: A unit used to measure frequency, the number of cycles, or sound waves, per second.

oscilloscope: An electronic instrument that converts pitch and frequency into pictures of the sound waves on a display screen.

partials: In music, the extra tones in a musical note that go with the dominant or fundamental tone to create an instrument's characteristic sound.

pitch: In music, the sound frequency of a note or tone.

refraction: The bending of a sound wave.

resonance: Vibration at the same frequency as a sound or musical note.

synthesizer: An electronic instrument that creates sounds.

ultrasound: Sound at frequencies higher than twenty thousand hertz—too high for the human ear to hear.

vibration: Rapid movement back and forth.